SO YOU THINK YOU KNOW CANADA, EH?

FASCINATING FUN FACTS AND TRIVIA ABOUT CANADA FOR THE ENTIRE FAMILY

MARIANNE JENNINGS

D1421937

Edited by
VALERIE BUCKNER

KNOWLEDGE NUGGETS SERIES

Copyright and Disclaimer

So You Think You Know CANADA, Eh?
Fascinating Fun Facts and Trivia about Canada for the Entire Family

Knowledge Nuggets Series by Marianne Jennings

Copyright © 2019 Knowledge Nugget Books
www.knowledgenuggetbooks.com
Bountiful, Utah

For permissions contact: hello@knowledgenuggetbooks.com

Edited by Valerie Buckner
Cover design: Anisha Umĕlec
Cover images used under license from Shutterstock.com

While all attempts have been made to verify the information provided in this publication, neither the author nor the publisher assumes any responsibility for errors, omissions, or contrary interpretations on the subject matter herein. This book is for entertainment purposes only. The views expressed are those of the author alone, and should not be taken as expert instruction or commands. The reader is responsible for his or her own actions.

Library of Congress Control Number: 2019917946
ISBN 9781734245615 (paperback)
ISBN 9781734245608 (ebook)

Trademarks that are mentioned are done without written consent and can in no way be considered an endorsement from the trademark holder.

Disclaimer: No Canadians were harmed during the making of this book.

For my mom, who is the smartest and wisest person I know. Thank you for encouraging me to never stop learning and for making it fun.

HOW TO READ THIS BOOK

This book is divided by topics that makes it easy to jump to wherever you'd like.

There is no need to read this book cover to cover.

Just pick a subject that seems interesting and dig right in.

Quiz Yourself
To test yourself and your friends with what you've learned, you'll find a fun, short quiz with answers in the back.

Please Bookmark the RESOURCES Page
so you can easily access all the videos, recipes, and other resources mentioned throughout this book with direct links to each.
KnowledgeNuggetBooks.com/resources

TABLE OF CONTENTS

FREE BONUS

As a **special bonus** and as a **thank you** for downloading this book, I created a **FREE companion quiz e-book** with **over 100 fun questions and answers** taken from this book.

How well DO YOU REALLY KNOW Canada?
Test your knowledge of Canada and quiz your friends.

It's all FREE.
Download your bonus quiz e-book here:

http://bit.ly/canada-bonus

Enjoy!

INTRODUCTION

When I think of Canada, I think of friendly and polite people, a variety of breathtaking landscapes, the Northern Lights, polar bears, Santa Claus, and maple syrup.

I have long been fascinated by Canada and everything that it has to offer. To help spread the love of this wonderful country and its delightful people, I've created what I hope to be an entertaining book filled with fun facts, interesting tidbits, and short stories.

It's my belief that when we learn more about other people and places, it opens up our hearts and our perspectives and makes our lives so much richer.

Here's hoping you learn a few things, laugh a little, and find a few fun facts to share with others.

CANADA - BASIC FACTS

CANADA'S NAME AND WHAT IT MEANS: The word "Canada" comes from the word "Kanata," a North American Indian (Huron) word meaning "village" or "settlement" in their Iroquoian language.

Legend has it that when the French explorer Jacques Cartier was meeting the native people in 1535, they invited him to come visit "Kanata" or, in other words, their village. He thought it meant the name of the entire land and the name stuck.

OTHER NAMES IN THE RUNNING: Not everyone wanted the country to be named Canada. In 1867, several alternative names were proposed. Here are just a handful with their meanings:

- **Britannia** - Another name for Britain.
- **Borealia** - Borealis is Latin for "Northern."
- **Cabotia** - Named after the Italian explorer, John Cabot, who explored and mapped out the eastern coast of Canada for England.

- **Efisga** - In order to represent all of the people in the land, this acronym was created by using the first letter of each: "**E**nglish, **F**rench, **I**rish, **S**cottish, **G**erman, and **A**boriginal."
- **Transatlantica** - Crossing the Atlantic.
- **Victorialand** - In honor of Queen Victoria.
- **Superior** - "Higher in rank, status, or quality."

WE MADE IT TO ASIA! OH WAIT... The Italian explorer John Cabot, who landed in Canada in 1498, originally thought he had arrived in Asia.

CANADA'S QUEEN. Queen Elizabeth II of England is also the Queen of Canada and the head of the state. Canadians can order a portrait of Queen Elizabeth II and have it shipped to them for free.

ELECTED BY THE PEOPLE. As of 2019, the current prime minister elected by the people is Justin Trudeau. Before he became the prime mister in 2015, Justin Trudeau had a variety of jobs including working as a nightclub bouncer and a snow-boarding instructor.

HOW CANADA IS DIVIDED UP. There are ten provinces and three territories in Canada.

THE LANGUAGES OF CANADA. Canada has two official languages: English and French. Almost half of the population can speak both languages. In the province of Quebec, French is spoken by more than 90 percent of the population. In fact, after Paris, the Canadian city of Montreal is the second largest French-speaking city in the world.

NATIONAL SYMBOLS. Canada's national symbols are the

maple leaf, the beaver, Canada goose, common loon, the Crown, the Royal Canadian Mounted Police, the totem pole, and Inuksuk (a man-made stone landmark or cairn).

THE FLAG OF CANADA. After 40 years of discussions and thousands of designs, a decision was finally made and Canada's red and white flag was raised for the first time on February 15, 1965.

The maple leaf has been used as a Canadian symbol since the 18th century. The red maple leaf featured on the flag has 11 points, but have no special meaning. However, the flag colors are symbolic. The red is symbolic of England and the white represents France.

CANADA'S MOTTO: "A Mari Usque Ad Mare", which means "From Sea to Sea" in English, was inspired by a passage in the Latin Vulgate version of the Old Testament in Psalms 72:8 in the Bible.

The full verse reads, "He shall have dominion also from sea to sea, and from the river unto the ends of the earth."

To be more inclusive of the Arctic portion of Canada, the motto is often accepted as "From Sea to Sea to Sea."

O CANADA. The song, "O Canada" was first performed on June 24, 1880 in Quebec City. It didn't become the official national anthem until a hundred years later on July 1, 1980.

Before "O Canada" was made the national anthem, "God Save the Queen" was the official national anthem, but "O Canada" and "The Maple Leaf Forever" were often used unofficially. "God Save the Queen" is still the royal anthem of Canada.

O Canada!
Our home and native land!
True patriot love in all thy sons command.
With glowing hearts we see thee rise,
The True North strong and free!
From far and wide,
O Canada, we stand on guard for thee.
God keep our land glorious and free!
O Canada, we stand on guard for thee.
O Canada, we stand on guard for thee.

IMPRESSIVE GEOGRAPHY FACTS

CANADA IS HUGE. Canada is the largest country in the Western hemisphere and the second largest country in the world, right after Russia, but only 0.5% of the world's population live there.

From north to south, Canada spans more than half of the Northern Hemisphere and measures 2,858 miles or 4,600 kilometers in total. From east to west, the country stretches across six time zones and is 3,417 miles, or 5,500 kilometers, wide.

BIGGER THAN THE USA. Canada is bigger, but just 1.5% bigger in land mass.

HIGHEST POINT. The highest point in Canada is at the summit of Canada's tallest mountain, Mount Logan. It stands at 19,551 feet or 5,959 meters above sea level and is still growing by an average of a few millimeters each year.

Mount Logan is the second-highest peak in North America, just after Denali in Alaska.

Mount Logan is taller than the tallest peak in Africa, Mount Kilimanjaro, which stands at 19,341 feet or 5,895 meters.

LARGEST MOUNTAIN. Mount Logan may not be the tallest mountain in the world, but it may be the *largest* in the world. Its overall footprint covers a larger area than any other mountain on Earth.

The 149-mile or 240-kilometer base is surrounded by glaciers and can only be circumnavigated on skies.

THAT'S ONE BIG ISLAND. Baffin Island is part of the Nunavut territory and is the fifth biggest island on earth. Only two U.S. states, Alaska and Texas, are bigger than Baffin Island.

ARCTIC CIRCLE ISLANDS. Most of Canada's northern islands are inside the Arctic Circle.

THE FROZEN CHOSEN AT THE TOP OF THE WORLD. The world's northernmost inhabited settlement is Alert, Nunavut, found at the northern tip of Ellesmere Island. Alert gets its unique name from the ship HMS *Alert*, which was the first to reach the north end of Ellesmere Island in 1875.

Around 65 people live in Alert and they call themselves the **"Frozen Chosen."** Most of these people are scientists and military personnel who work at the Canadian Forces Station Alert, a weather station, a Global Atmosphere Watch laboratory, and a military airport.

In July, the warmest month, the average temperatures are 38° Fahrenheit or 3.4° Celsius. In January, the coldest month has average temperatures around -26° Fahrenheit or -32° Celsius.

LAND OF LAKES. Canada has more lakes than the rest of the world's lakes combined. Ontario, Canada has more than 250,000 lakes. These lakes contain about one-fifth or 20% of the world's fresh water.

BIGGEST LAKES IN THE WORLD. Two of the biggest lakes in the world are in Canada. They are the Great Bear Lake and the Great Slave Lake.

LARGEST COASTLINE. Canada has the largest coastline in the world with 125,567 miles or 202,080 kilometers. To put that into perspective, if you were to walk around the Canadian coastline without stopping, it would take about 4.5 years.

WORLD'S HIGHEST TIDES. The highest tidal range in the world is found in The Bay of Fundy in the eastern part of Canada. The difference between low tide and high tide has been up to 53 feet or 16 meters, which is taller than a three-story building.

The Bay of Fundy is one of the 7 wonders of North America, not only because of the highest tides, but because it is a temporary home to some of the rarest whales in the world. These are the North Atlantic right whales, the sei whales (one of the world's fastest marine animals), and True's beaked whales.

HUDSON BAY. Hudson Bay is Canada's biggest bay and the second largest in the world. Since half of it is located inside the Arctic Circle, the bay frequently freezes ice up to 3 to 6.5 inches or 7.6 to 16.5 centimeters thick in the winter months, making it the perfect hunting ground for polar bears.

During the summer, it's home to more than 50,000 Beluga whales.

DID YOU KNOW?

In total, eight Canadian provinces and territories and thirteen U.S. states are located along the U.S./Canada border.

CRAZY CANADIAN WEATHER

CANADA IS THE COOLEST, SOMETIMES. Canada and Russia go back and forth on being the number 1 coldest nation in the world. Annual average daily temperatures are 21.9°F or -5.6°C.

AS COLD AS MARS. The coldest recorded temperature was -81.4°F or -63°C in 1947 in Snag, Yukon. The surface of Mars is roughly the same temperature.

Even colder record temperatures were measured on top of Canada's tallest mountain. In 1991, on top of Mount Logan, the temperature measured -108° Fahrenheit or -77.5° Celsius.

This is the lowest recorded temperature for the northern hemisphere and outside of Antarctica. Before Canada broke this record, Siberia had the lowest recorded temperature in the northern hemisphere at -90° Fahrenheit or -68° Celsius.

CANADA'S COLD CAPITAL. In January 2019, Ottawa broke

the world record with temperatures of -11.2 °F or -24 °C and became the coldest capital in the world.

On average though, the capital of Mongolia, Ulan Bator, holds the number one spot with winter temperatures normally around -13°F or -20°C.

HOT, HOT, HOT. The hottest recorded temperature was 113° Fahrenheit or 45° Celsius in Saskatchewan in July 1937.

DON'T LIKE THE WEATHER? WAIT FIVE MINUTES. If you've ever been to Canada, you may have experienced a wide range of temperatures within a single day.

The most extreme temperature change was recorded in Pincher Creek, Alberta in 1962, where, in just one hour, it went from -2° F to 72° F or -19°C to 22°C.

THE LARGEST WAVE. The largest wave height ever recorded was on September 11, 1995, off the coast of Newfoundland.

A 98.4 foot or 30-meter wave hit the QE2 ocean liner when it was caught in Hurricane Luis. This storm was so gigantic; it covered almost the entire North Atlantic.

WHEN THE OCEAN FREEZES. In Newfoundland, the Atlantic Ocean sometimes freezes, so naturally, they do what Canadians do when a body of water freezes: they play ice hockey on it.

DID YOU KNOW?

THE GREAT CANADIAN FOG

The Grand Banks of Newfoundland is not only considered one of the richest fishing grounds in the world, but also the foggiest place in the world.

WORLD RECORD-BREAKING FACTS & STATS

LONGEST HIGHWAY. The longest highway in the world is the Trans-Canada Highway, which measures 4,275 miles or 7,608 kilometers long.

It runs from the Pacific Ocean on the west through all ten Canadian provinces to the Atlantic Ocean on the east.

LONGEST STREET. The longest street in the world is the Yonge Street in Ontario, Canada at 1,178 miles or 1,896 km long.

TALLEST BUILDING. Until 2007, the CN Tower in Toronto, Ontario held the world record for being the largest freestanding structure for more than three decades. It is the tallest in the western hemisphere and is one of the Seven Wonders of the Modern World. It is 1,815.3 feet or 553.3 meters tall.

LONGEST BORDER. Canada and the U.S. share the longest international border in the world. It's officially known as the International Boundary and is 5,525 miles or 8,891 km long and includes the 1,538 mile or 2,891 km Canada's border with Alaska.

In total, eight Canadian provinces and territories and thirteen U.S. states are located along the border.

LARGEST TOTEM POLE. At one time, "The World's Largest Totem Pole" was found in Alert Bay, British Columbia.

It was built from two sections, the main one being 163 feet or 49.6 meters tall and the spire, being 10 feet or 3 meters.

It stood 173 feet or 53 meters tall and included symbolic figures of the Sun Man, a whale, an old man, a wolf, the Thunderbird and its cousin, the Kulusl, a two-headed serpent, a bear holding a salmon, and a raven holding copper.

The title of "The World's Largest Totem Pole" is greatly disputed and has been claimed by several different Pacific Northwest towns. Disagreements are based on whether or not the pole was carved from one or multiple wood pieces and whether or not it was carved by an indigenous artisan.

OLYMPIC RECORDS. Canada set a new record for the most gold medals (14) won by a country in a single Winter Olympics in Vancouver in 2010.

Canada won the gold medal in the very first ice hockey event held in the 1920 Olympic Games.

KIND & SMART

POSITIVE TICKETS. When people are seen doing something positive, the Canadian Police Department in Vancouver may reward them by giving them "positive tickets." These are normally a voucher or coupon to some fun activity.

OPERATION YELLOW RIBBON. When flights were diverted or grounded during the 9/11 terrorist attack, Canada housed, fed, and sheltered more than 33,000 passengers from over 224 planes in what is now known as Operation Yellow Ribbon.

To learn more and to see one of the finest examples of the grace and generosity of the Canadian people, this video is worth watching. TV journalist and author Tom Brokaw produced this video about Operation Yellow Ribbon. Watch it here: https://youtu.be/jXbxoy4Mges

FRIENDLY & POLITE. Canadians are considered as one of the friendliest and most polite people in the world. According to a 2016 InterNations expat survey report, Canada was ranked as one of the safest, most welcoming, and best countries to make friends.

In an Ipsos Reid and Historica Canada poll in 2014, 92% of Canadians believe that Canadians are polite people. In 2015, Canada was named the number one country with the best reputation by the Reputation Institute.

CANADIAN SWEET TWEETS. A study by two McMaster University doctoral students showed that Canadians are nicer than Americans on Twitter.

More than 3 million tweets were analyzed and it showed that overall Canadians use more positive words like "great", "amazing" and "beautiful" throughout their tweets. Americans use more vulgar and coarse language in their tweets overall.

IF YOU'RE NOT NICE, SOMEONE MIGHT DIE. Canada's harsh winters are rough and to survive, Canadians look out for each other. For example, if your car breaks down in the winter on the side of the road and the next person coming along doesn't stop, you're in a dangerous situation. Canadians are more likely to stop and help.

NICENESS IN ACTION. Examples of Canadian niceness can easily be found in the Canadian Press. In Edmonton, the National Post reported that a law student left his headlights on all day. When he returned to his car, he found his battery dead and a note on his windshield.

The note read, "I noticed you left your lights on. The battery will probably not have enough charge to start your vehicle. I left a blue extension cord on the fence and … a battery charger beside the fence in a cardboard box." The note gave instructions on how to jump-start the vehicle and was signed off with "Good luck."

POLAR BEAR SAFETY. If you're in Churchill, Manitoba in northern Canada and run into a polar bear, you can escape by finding the closest car and getting in. It's normal for residents to leave their cars unlocked to offer an escape for this exact situation.

WELL-EDUCATED. Canada tops the list as the most educated country in the world. At least 56% of its residents have college degrees with Japan coming in at second place with 50%.

LITERACY SKILLS. Canada's literacy rate is 99% which means that almost all Canadians can read and write.

CANADA'S WILD AND RUGGED NATURE

CANADA WAS THE FIRST COUNTRY TO CREATE A NATIONAL PARK SERVICE. While Canada was not the first to create a national park, it was the first to create a national park service dedicated to protecting them.

CANADA HAS 47 NATIONAL PARKS. Banff National Park was Canada's first national park and the third national park in the world. It opened in 1885. Technically, there are 39 National Parks and 8 National Park Reserves, as of 2019.

SOME OF CANADA'S NATIONAL PARKS ARE BIGGER THAN SOME COUNTRIES. The Nahanni National Park Reserve in the Northwest Territories, known for its massive waterfalls, is bigger than Albania and Israel.

Even bigger is the Wood Buffalo National Park in Alberta and the Northwest Territories, which is bigger than Denmark and Switzerland.

CANADA'S LARGEST NATIONAL PARK. Wood Buffalo Park isn't just the largest in Canada, it's the second-largest national park in the world. The only bigger national park is Greenland's Northeast Greenland National Park.

KIDS GET IN FREE. National parks in Canada are free for kids and youth under 18 years of age, permanently.

CANADA HAS 19 UNESCO WORLD HERITAGE SITES. There are 9 cultural sites, 9 natural sites, and 1 mixed site recognized by the United Nations. Head-Smashed-In Buffalo Jump is the one with the most unique name.

HEAD-SMASHED-IN BUFFALO JUMP. This UNESCO World Heritage site is one of the oldest and best-preserved buffalo jumps in the world.

A very long time ago, the Blackfoot people would kill buffalo by driving them off the 36-foot-high or 11-meter-high cliffs.

According to one legend, the name of the site comes from a story of a young Blackfoot who wanted to watch as the buffalo tumbled past.

He chose the wrong place to watch and was buried underneath the fallen buffalo and was found with his head smashed in.

DID YOU KNOW?
NORTHERN LIGHTS
One of the best places in the world to see the northern lights is in Yellowknife, the capital city of Canada's Northwest Territories.

The best time to see them is from mid-August till the end of September and from mid-November until mid-April.

ANIMAL FACTS

BEAVERS, BUFFALO, AND DEER, OH MY! Canada is home to many different types of animals and wildlife. You can find bears, wolves, buffalo, antelope, deer, mountain lions, beavers, bighorn sheep as well as raccoons, otters, and rabbits. Up in northern Canada, you'll find moose, caribou, musk ox, and polar bears.

WILD BEARS. Canada is home to the biggest population of several types of wild bears. Black bears, grizzlies, and Kermode bears are found in large numbers all around Canada. Of the 25,000 polar bears in the world, around 15,000 live in the northern parts of Canada.

SNAKE NIGHTMARE OR DREAM COME TRUE? Like snakes? If so, you will find the largest snake pit in the world filled with garter snakes in Manitoba, Canada.

If snakes are your worst nightmare, these countries have no snakes at all: New Zealand, Ireland, Iceland, and Greenland.

100% RAT-FREE. Hate rats? Alberta, Canada has been rat-free for more than 50 years. Rats, especially brown Norway rats, are one of the most destructive creatures known to man. They contaminate food, weaken buildings and carry diseases.

Rats are not native to North America but were brought in around the time of the American Revolution in 1775. The rats made their way north and crossed into Alberta in 1950.

The Alberta government had a plan in place in case this ever happened and were able to quickly and effectively halt the infestation. Their rat control program has proved to be the most successful in the world.

CANADA'S NATIONAL ANIMAL FACTS

FEATURED ON THE FIVE-CENT COIN. The North American beaver is the national animal of Canada. The beaver has been an important part of Canada's history and was a big part in the fur trade. To honor the beaver, it is featured on Canada's five-cent coin.

HOME & FAMILY LIFE. Beavers are very social and live in groups called colonies. Beavers are monogamous and baby beavers are called kits. Beaver dams are built with mud and wood which creates a still, deep area of water that protects beaver colonies from wolves, bears, and eagles.

Beaver homes are built in the middle of the dam and are called lodges. The dome-shaped lodges have two dens and an underwater entrance. The first den is used to dry off and the second den is dryer and is where a family of up to four adults and six to eight kits live.

BEAVER TEETH. Beavers are known for their large front teeth. These teeth never stop growing. To keep their teeth from growing too long beavers are almost always gnawing on wood. Because their front teeth stick out in front of their lips, beavers can cut and chew wood underwater without getting water in their mouths.

ALARM SYSTEM. Beavers use their big, broad tails to signal danger in the area to other beavers by loudly slapping the water.

IMPRESSIVE SWIMMERS & BUILT-IN GOGGLES. Their webbed feet don't allow beavers to move fast on dry land but make it possible to swim very fast in the water. A beaver can stay underwater for up to 15 minutes. Beavers have transparent eyelids that act like goggles and make it possible for them to see underwater.

BIG BEAVERS. Beavers are Canada's largest rodent and the second-largest rodent in the world. They can weigh up to 60 pounds or 27.2 kilograms. In case you're curious, the largest rodent in the world is the capybara, which is found in South America and can weigh up to 100 pounds or 45.3 kilograms.

LITTLE KNOWN CARIBOU FACTS

COUNTING CARIBOU. Canada has almost 2.5 million caribou. Caribou and reindeer are the same species, but there are a few differences; Caribou are normally larger, wilder, and elk-like.

Caribou have never been domesticated.

REINDEER OR CARIBOU? To make matters more confusing, caribou are called reindeer in Russia and Scandinavia. Everywhere else, however, these wild animals are known as caribou.

ALL CARIBOU HAVE ANTLERS. Caribou are the only species in the deer family where both the male and the female have antlers.

The female's antlers are smaller than the male's, but they carry them longer. Caribou start growing their antlers in the spring. Male caribou lose their antlers in November or December. Female caribou, especially those who have had babies, don't lose their antlers until June. This helps them to protect their calves.

BULLS AND COWS. Male caribou are called bulls and weigh around 330 pounds or 150 kilograms. Female caribou are called cows and weigh around 209 pounds or 95 kilograms.

Baby caribou are called calves. Caribou only have one calf per year.

DID YOU KNOW?

Canada's 25-cent coin has the caribou on one side.

8

HOLIDAYS & TRADITIONS

HERE ARE JUST A FEW OF CANADA'S FAVORITE
HOLIDAYS AND FUN TRADITIONS.

CANADA DAY. The national holiday of Canada is celebrated on July 1st, marking the day in 1867 when the original three colonies of Canada united into a single nation.

This day was previously known as Dominion Day until 1983. Canadians celebrate with good food, parades, fireworks, and other patriotic activities.

VICTORIA DAY. Queen Victoria was well loved throughout her empire and when she died, the Canadian Parliament declared her birthday, May 24, a Canadian national holiday.

It's now been over a hundred years and the holiday has evolved into a day to celebrate the current monarch (Queen Elizabeth II).

Instead of being on the same day each year, Victoria Day is celebrated on the Monday nearest the 24th, which makes for an extended weekend. It's often referred to as "May Long."

NATIONAL INDIGENOUS PEOPLES DAY. Formerly known as Aboriginal Day, this is a yearly celebration on June 21st which often falls on the summer solstice, an occasion that is special to many of the indigenous people.

It's a day to celebrate and recognize their culture, accomplishments, and unique heritage.

There are three different aboriginal groups in Canada - First Nation, Inuit, and Métis. It's not just a day for Indigenous people, it's a chance for all Canadians to learn more about their culture and history.

Members of the public are often invited to attend pow wows, festivals, dances, ceremonies and parades held all over the country.

HALLOWEEN & FIREWORKS. Halloween is a big deal in Canada. One of the ways they celebrate is by setting off fireworks.

In Vancouver, Halloween is the only day of the year where people can legally set off fireworks in their backyards. Permits are obtained and Halloween in Vancouver is a spectacular sight.

CANADIAN THANKSGIVING. Canadians celebrate Thanksgiving just like Americans, but they celebrate on the second Monday in October, rather than in November.

The very first Thanksgiving celebration in North America took place in Canada in 1578 more than 40 years earlier than the first American Thanksgiving in 1621.

THE STAMPEDE. The Calgary Stampede, an annual rodeo that takes place over several days, is known as the "The Greatest Outdoor Show on Earth."

More than one million people from around the world visit to "preserve and celebrate western heritage, culture and community spirit." They celebrate through rodeo events with big prize money, concerts, carnival rides, a parade, and agricultural competitions.

DID YOU KNOW?

More than 200,000 pancakes are served during Calgary's Stampede.

All of them are free.

The Flapjack Finder app was created to make it easy to find Calgary Stampede flapjack breakfasts near you during the 10-day festival.

9

SANTA AND THE NORTH POLE

LETTERS TO SANTA. Every Christmas, Santa Claus receives around one million letters from around the world, even as far away as New Zealand or South Africa.

Santa Claus has his own special mailing address with his very own postal code. Send your letters to:

Santa Claus
North Pole, H0H 0H0
Canada

In case you didn't notice, Santa's unique zip/postal code **H0H 0H0** is extra special because it reads as "Ho ho ho."

SANTA SPEAKS ALL THE LANGUAGES. It doesn't matter what language you send your letters in, Santa answers the letters in the same language in which they are sent. Some years, this means it's close to 200 different languages.

DID YOU KNOW?
SANTA IS OFFICIALLY CANADIAN.
In 2008, Santa was declared a Canadian citizen by Canada's Immigration Minister.

10

PEOPLE & POPULATION

ROOM TO SPREAD OUT. Even though Canada is the second-largest country in the world, it has one of the lowest population densities. Only 10% of Canada's land is inhabited.

Think of it this way, Canada is only slightly larger than the U.S. but only has 11% of America's population.

Canada has fewer people than Tokyo's metropolitan area. As of 2019, Canada's population was estimated at 37.06 million. Tokyo's metro area was estimated at 37.83 million.

WHERE MOST CANADIANS LIVE. Nine out of ten Canadians live near the U.S.-Canada border.

LIFE EXPECTANCY. The average life expectancy in Canada is 81 years, which is the sixth highest in the world.

CANADA'S ORIGINAL INHABITANTS. Three different groups, referred to as Aboriginal Canadians, are the country's original inhabitants.

About 1.4 million are First Nation, Metis, and Inuit and each group has their own history and cultures. June 21st is celebrated as National Aboriginal Day in Canada.

ANCIENT INVENTIONS. The canoe, kayak, cough syrup, darts, and lacrosse all come from the people who have been in Canada for at least 12,000 years.

MULTICULTURAL. Canada is a melting pot of people and cultures. For example, in Toronto, more than 140 different languages are spoken and almost 50% of people were born outside of Canada.

CANADIAN NEWCOMERS. Immigrants make up nearly 22% of the population of Canada. The top newcomers come from the Philippines, China, India, and the U.S.

DID YOU KNOW?

"Li" is the most common last name in Canada according to a report published by CBC News in 2007.

11

CANADA & SPORTS

HOCKEY. Canada is considered to be the birthplace of ice hockey. The first organized indoor hockey game was played in Montreal in 1875.

While hockey is the sport most closely associated with Canada, lacrosse, a First Nations game, is the official sport of Canada.

HOCKEY PUCKS. The first hockey pucks used in the 1800s was frozen cow dung. These days, the hockey pucks are made of black vulcanized rubber and are 3 inches wide and 1 inch thick.

To make it so they don't bounce during a game they are frozen before the game. On average, 12 brand-new, frozen pucks are used in an NHL game.

UNDERWATER HOCKEY. While underwater hockey was invented in England, the first Underwater Hockey World Championship was held in Canada in 1980.

Underwater hockey is also called Octopush and is a globally

played sport. Players use a small hockey stick to get a weighted puck into the opposing team's goal all while swimming along the bottom of a pool.

Underwater Hockey was first introduced to Canada in Vancouver in 1962. The Canadian Underwater Games Association was created and Canada now has several national teams for not only underwater hockey, but underwater rugby.

For those interested, learn more at http://cuga.org/en/ or check out this video: https://youtu.be/dhs8jfy-A6o

LACROSSE. Lacrosse has been around since the 1700s and is considered the oldest team sport in North America.

It's a First Nations game that not only brought different tribes and villages together, but was also used to prepare young men for war.

Lacrosse has become popular worldwide and is played in more than 50 countries, including Jamaica, Latvia, and China.

SOCCER. For Canadian youth under 14, soccer is the most played sport. Twice as many kids play soccer than hockey.

DOWNHILL SKIING. If you like to downhill ski, there are over 280 ski resorts in Canada. Whistler, British Columbia is ranked as one of the best places to ski in North America.

HELISKIING. Adrenaline junkies may find it interesting that heliskiing was born in Canada and over 90 percent of the world's heliskiing is done in British Columbia.

SNOWMOBILING. Not only is snowmobiling or snowmachining, as they say in northern Canada, a very popular Canadian outdoor activity it's also the main form of winter transportation in some areas. There are over 610,000 registered snowmobiles with 1.5 million family members snowmobiling in Canada.

FISHING. Since Canada has more lakes then the rest of the world's lake combined, it makes sense that fishing would be a popular Canadian sport.

Canada even has an entire week dedicated to fishing each year to encourage Canadians to build memories with friends and loved ones and to foster a passion and respect for the outdoors. According to Fisheries and Oceans Canada, almost one in ten Canadians went fishing in 2017.

ICE FISHING. Fishing in Canada is a year-round activity. A few things to remember when ice fishing in Canada; if using an ice hut, it must be registered and that it is illegal to leave your ice fishing hole uncovered.

CURLING. This Olympic sport involves ice, round rocks sliding across the ice, sweeping, wearing two different shoes, and is the only sport where players shake hands at the beginning and the end of every game. This fun video shows a quick overview: https://youtu.be/WXHh_wadqPw

It's also known as "Chess on Ice" due to the strategy involved and "The Roaring Game" because of the sound the rare granite stones make sliding on the ice.

Curling was born in Scotland and was brought to Canada by Scottish emigrants. Curling has only been an official medal Olympic sport since the 1998 Olympic Games.

Curling is a big deal in Canada and they even hold the record for winning the most Olympic medals for curling with a total of 11. The first indoor ice rink in Canada was built for curling, not hockey.

OLYMPIC GAMES. Canada has hosted the Olympic Games **three times**: the 1976 Summer Olympics in Montreal, the 1988 Winter Olympics in Calgary, and the 2010 Winter Olympics in Vancouver.

CANADA ALWAYS COMPETES. Since 1900, Canada has sent athletes to every Winter Olympics and every Summer Olympics (except one in 1980 in Moscow, which they boycotted along with 65 other nations, protesting the 1979 Soviet invasion of Afghanistan).

MEDAL WINNERS. Canada has won at least one medal at every Olympics the country has competed in.

DID YOU KNOW?

In Vancouver, you can ski, golf, bike, sail, and kayak all in the same day.

12

FAMOUS INVENTIONS MADE BY CANADIANS

SPORTS & GAMES

BASKETBALL. Dr. James Naismith, a Canadian native, was in charge of creating an indoor winter game for college students in Massachusetts. He wanted to create a game that required skill and not strength.

He was inspired by a game he played as a teenager called duck-on-a-rock, that involved trying to knock a "duck" off the top of a large rock by throwing another rock at it.

The first ever game of basketball was played in 1891 using a soccer ball and two peach baskets for the hoops.

ICE HOCKEY. There's a lot of debate as to where the game of hockey originated. Some say Nova Scotia, while others say Europe should be recognized as the birthplace of hockey.

What we do know is that the first officially organized, indoor game of hockey was played in Montreal.

THE HOCKEY GOALIE MASK. There's also some debate over exactly who invented the goalie mask. It was something that has evolved over time.

In 1927, Elizabeth Graham, a goaltender for Ontario's Queen's University hockey team was the first person to wear a mask on the ice by donning a fencing mask to protect her teeth.

In 1930, Clint Benedict wore a leather mask a few times to protect his face while on the ice.

Goalie Jacque Plante, in 1959, had a fiberglass mask made and used it during practice. After getting hit in the face during a game, he refused to go back out on the ice without the mask. Since then, goalies have worn masks to protect their faces.

LACROSSE. Versions of the game of lacrosse have been around for hundreds of years and the sport is considered the oldest game in North America.

It wasn't until 1856 that a Canadian dentist created what we now know as the game of lacrosse. He created the first lacrosse club, established standard rules, standardized the length of play, and used 12 players per team.

TABLE HOCKEY. During the Depression, a Toronto man got creative when coming up with a Christmas gift for his family.

He used a variety of items from around his house such as clothes pins, wire hangers, clock springs, and lumber and created what is now known as table hockey.

TRIVIAL PURSUIT GAME. One evening in 1979, two friends in Montreal couldn't find all of their tiles for a game of Scrabble. Instead of calling it a night, they got creative and came up with their own game and called it Trivial Pursuit.

This trivia board game has gone on to be added to the "Games Hall of Fame" and was sold to Hasbro for $80 million dollars. As of 2019, over 100 million games have been sold around the world.

FOOD RELATED

THE EGG CARTON. Before the egg carton, eggs were delivered in baskets, and often arrived broken. The egg carton made delivering fresh eggs without cracking their fragile shells much easier.

It was invented in 1911 by a Canadian newspaper publisher who came up with a way to hold eggs in individual, cushioned pockets.

INSTANT MASHED POTATOES. Just add hot water to these dried potato flakes and you've got instant mashed potatoes. These were invented in Canada in 1962, to be fast and easy meals for weekend campers and for the military.

PEANUT BUTTER. A Montreal pharmacist invented peanut butter when he wanted to make a tasty food option for people who couldn't chew. The first patent for peanut butter was awarded in 1884.

MCINTOSH APPLES, NOT COMPUTERS. McIntosh apples are Canada's national apple, named after the man who discovered the native seedlings on his land in 1811, John McIntosh. He gathered up the seeds and planted them near his home.

The fruit was perfect for cooking and eating and John and his family learned how to graft and grow more of these types of trees.

They began to sell them in 1835 and they quickly became very popular. Today, McIntosh apples make up 40% of Canada's apple market.

Apple, Inc. employee, Jef Raskin, named the first line of personal computers after his favorite fruit, which are now known as Macintosh or Mac computers. He deliberately misspelled the name so it would be slightly different and to avoid a conflict with the McIntosh Laboratory company.

COMMUNICATION

THE TELEPHONE. Alexander Graham Bell was born in Scotland but lived in Ontario when he invented the telephone in 1876.

THE WALKIE-TALKIE. A portable radio signaling system was invented in 1937 by Canadian inventor Donald Hings. It was originally called the "packset." The first model was not hand held, but was a pack worn on the back.

THE FOGHORN. Fog, boats, and rocky coastlines are a

dangerous combination. In 1854, the foghorn was invented in New Brunswick as a way to warn boats about hazards like rocky coastlines and other ships in foggy conditions.

SNOW RELATED

THE SNOWMOBILE. Invented in Quebec in 1935, the snowmobile made effective travel in snowy conditions possible.

Joseph-Armand Bombardier invented the first snowmobile and his first customers were country doctors, ambulance drivers, and priests who lived in remote areas.

THE SNOWBLOWER. The first snowblower, invented in Montreal in 1925, was a four-wheel drive truck that had the snowblower on the front to clear the streets. This first snowblower could throw snow up to 90 feet or 27.4 meters.

TRAIN TRACK SNOW PLOW. A rotary snow plow clears train tracks of snow using a large set of rotating blades and was invented by a Toronto dentist in 1869.

DID YOU KNOW?

The Zamboni, the vehicle used to resurface ice in ice rinks, was NOT invented in Canada. It was invented in California.

INVENTIONS FOR THE BODY

THE ARTIFICIAL PACEMAKER. The pacemaker is a device that has saved and prolonged many lives by using electrical impulses to regulate heartbeats.

If a heart is beating too fast, a pacemaker slows it down. If it is beating too slow, a pacemaker can increase the speed.

More than 1 million artificial pacemakers are implanted each year around the world. It was invented in 1950 at the University of Toronto's Banting Institute.

INSULIN. Technically, insulin wasn't invented since it's a hormone naturally produced by the pancreas.

But in 1922 at the University of Toronto, Dr. Frederick Banting and Charles Best identified the hormone and discovered it could be used to treat diabetes.

TRAVEL RELATED

BAGGAGE TAGS. The first baggage tags were stickers on trunks used on steamships and trains. In 1882, the modern baggage tag, which features a removable receipt to keep track of the owner, departure location, and final destination, was invented in Canada.

THE ELECTRIC WHEELCHAIR. Engineer George Kelin invented the electric wheelchair in Canada in 1952 in response to the many WWII veterans who returned from the war with serious injuries.

WHEELCHAIR-ACCESSIBLE BUS. Walter Harris Callow was a Canadian veteran who was blind and a quadriplegic.

While in the Camp Hill Hospital in Halifax, Nova Scotia, he invented the first wheelchair accessible bus in 1947.

This enabled those in wheelchairs, some who hadn't been outside in years due to lack of appropriate transportation, to get out and see the countryside, go on picnics, and attend sporting events.

The Callow Wheelchair Bus service continues today.

OTHER INTERESTING INVENTIONS

THE GREEN INK USED IN AMERICAN MONEY. The special green ink on U.S. dollar bills was invented by Thomas Sterry Hunt, a chemist, in Montreal in 1857.

This ink couldn't be destroyed by acid or be copied by photography, making it difficult to create counterfeit money.

At the time, photography was limited to black and white and forgers were unable to copy the color green.

THE PAINT ROLLER. In 1940, a Canadian invented the first paint roller. The first patent was filed by an American inventor, however, who took the original design and made a few design changes.

THE INSTANT REPLAY. Now a staple in sports, the first instant replay debuted in 1955 during a Hockey Night broadcast in Canada.

GARBAGE BAGS. The first garbage bags designed for commercial use were invented in 1950 in Ontario. These plastic, stretchy and waterproof bags were made for home use in the late 1960s under the name Glad Garbage Bags.

DID YOU KNOW?

Superman was created by Canadian-born artist Joe Shuster and Jerry Siegel, an American writer, in 1932.

13

RANDOM & AWESOME

CALL ME, MAYBE. Canada's official phone number is 1-800-O-CANADA.

POLAR BEAR LICENSE PLATES. The Canadian Northwest Territories license plates for cars, motorbikes, and snowmobiles are shaped like polar bears.

WHISKEY WAR. Since the 1930s, Canada and Denmark have been fighting a "whiskey war" over an uninhabited island by leaving each other bottles of alcohol and changing their flags.

Hans Island is an uninhabited half-square mile island located in a spot in the Arctic North claimed by both Canada and Denmark.

HAPPY CANADIANS. Canada is ranked as one of the happiest nations in the world. In the 2018 Happiness Report, Canada ranked number 7. In 2019, Canada ranked number 9.

For those who are curious, Finland has been ranked as the happiest nation in the world for two years in a row.

WINNIE-THE-POOH. An orphaned, black bear female cub was found and sold to a soldier as a pet in White River, Ontario. He named her Winnipeg after his hometown.

The soldier was transferred to Europe and knew he couldn't take care of his pet bear and made arrangements to keep her in the London Zoo in 1915, where she was known as Winnie.

Winnie was a crowd favorite and very tame. She would let children ride on her back and even eat from their hands.

She was adored by many including a little boy named Christopher Robin Milne who would visit the zoo with his father A.A. Milne.

Christopher received a stuffed bear as a birthday present and named her Winnie-the-Pooh.

A.A. Milne started writing children's stories based on the beloved bear at the zoo, his son, and his son's stuffed animals.

Christopher and his father came up with the bear's character name by including the name of a pet swan, Pooh. The rest, as they say, is history.

ARRESTED FOR CAUSING MISCHIEF. A Canadian man was arrested and charged for causing mischief after tying more than 100 helium balloons to a garden chair and flying over the city of Calgary in 2015.

Daniel Boria, 26, wanted to promote his cleaning-products company by parachuting into the Calgary Stampede.

After the balloons took him too high, he "somersaulted out the chair" and safely parachuted down and landed in a field just outside the city.

CANADIAN MOUNTIES. The name "Mounties" is actually a nickname given to the Royal Canadian Mounted Police or RCMP. Canadian Mounties are known for their bright red uniforms, the horses they ride and are one of the most iconic symbols of Canada.

Their famous red uniform is called the "Red Serge" and is usually only worn for ceremonial purposes. The scarlet color jacket was chosen in 1870 to differentiate them from the American blue uniforms. The hat is a wide-brimmed Stetson hat. The brown leather riding boots must shine and the trousers or pants are midnight blue, not black. The yellow stripe down the legs of the pants references its cavalry history. The cavalry were the soldiers who fought on horseback.

Unlike the name says, Canadian Mounties no longer serve on horses. They only use horses during ceremonial events.

BLIND-FRIENDLY BILLS. In Canada, bank notes have Braille-like raised markings on them that make them easily identifiable to the blind or low vision. Other countries who do this are Australia, Mexico, India, Russia, and Israel.

PLAYING CARDS AS MONEY. Due to a chronic shortage of coinage in 1685, playing cards were once used as currency in Canada.

CANADA'S SPACE PROGRAM. After the U.S. and the U.S.S.R., Canada was the third country in space. In 1962, Canada was considered to have the most advanced space program.

BLACK HOLE EVIDENCE. In 1972, researchers at the University of Toronto located a black hole for the first time.

Scientists, including Albert Einstein, had previously predicted the existence of black holes but the University of Toronto researchers, using a powerful telescope, were the first to identify one.

CANADARM I, II AND III. Three of Canada's greatest contributions to space exploration are the robotic arms Canadarm I, Canadarm II, and Canadarm III.

These remote-controlled arms help dock space shuttles, capture and deploy satellites, and even helped build the International Space Station itself.

CANADIAN PASSPORT SECRETS. The newest Canadian passports have hidden symbols and graphics on the inside pages that only appear under black light.

What looks like a normal passport page transforms into technicolor designs with fireworks, colorful maple leaves, and Niagara Falls.

Here's a video showing what each page looks like with and without the blacklight. https://youtu.be/mvRAqmju3wc

CANADIAN PASSPORTS & FREE BEER. As a marketing campaign, Molson Beer, a Canadian beer company, created custom refrigerators and stocked them full of Molson Beer in different places all over Europe.

Only someone with a Canadian Passport can scan their passport and open the fridge.

DID YOU KNOW?

Before the U.S. Constitution was in place, there were the Articles of Confederation.

In one of the thirteen articles, Canada had an open invite to be admitted into the U.S. automatically and with no strings attached. This is no longer the case.

14

THE TITANIC AND THE HALIFAX CONNECTION

AFTER THE TITANIC SANK. When the Titanic sank in 1912, Halifax, Nova Scotia, located on the eastern coast of Canada, was the closest port city to the tragedy.

All but five of the 334 recovered bodies from the Titanic sinking were retrieved by Canadian ships. 125 of those bodies were buried at sea due to severe damage, advanced decomposition, or lack of supplies like embalming fluid. The remaining 209 of the 334 recovered bodies were taken to Halifax to be identified.

NEW SYSTEM INVENTED. The Halifax coroner, Dr. John Henry Barnstead, was tasked with identifying the 209 bodies recovered after the *Titanic* tragedy and came up with a system for identifying mass casualties that is still used today.

About two-thirds of the recovered bodies were identified using this brand-new system.

Bodies were numbered as they were pulled from the sea and

their personal effects were kept in small canvas bags with matching numbers.

Details like tattoos, clothes, and jewelry were carefully noted and photographs were taken.

Due to the detailed records that were kept and which are still available, six previously unidentified *Titanic* victims were identified in 1992.

The majority of recovered victims that arrived in Halifax are buried in three Halifax cemeteries.

15

INTERESTING WAR HISTORY

AMERICAN INVADERS. Americans have invaded Canada twice, once in 1775 and again in 1812. Both times, the Americans lost.

CANADA DECLARED WAR FIRST. Hours after the attack on Pearl Harbor on Dec. 7, 1941, during World War II, Canada declared war on Japan. The U.S. and Great Britain joined them a day later and declared war on Japan on Dec. 8, 1941.

THE APPLICANT FOR ENLISTMENT PIN. During World War II, some Canadians who tried to enlist in the Canadian Forces were turned away for medical reasons. Canada gave out special pins to honor and recognize their willingness to fight.

THE DEVIL'S BRIGADE. In 1942, 1,800 Americans and Canadians came together in this joint special force unit to take on critical missions in World War II from Italy to France.

They disbanded at the end of the war, but the Devil's Brigade became the special forces operation model for both Canadian and American special forces, like the Green Berets, the SEALs, Joint Task Force 2 (JTF2), and the Canadian Special Operations Regiment (CSOR).

POWS REQUESTED TO STAY IN CANADA. During World War II, there were more than 35,000 prisoners of war held in 27 "prison camps" across Canada. While they were called prison camps, they weren't run like the average prison camp.

Prisoners were given nice clothing, stayed in dormitories, were well fed in dining halls, and had access to recreation centers where they could play football, handball, wrestle, or skate. They had access to books and education, organized their own band and orchestra, and held paid jobs.

After the war ended, more than 6,000 prisoners were so pleased with how they were treated that they asked to stay in Canada rather than return to Europe.

THE "BIRTHPLACE" OF JAMES BOND. During World War II, a real secret agent training camp in Ontario, known as Camp X, trained secret agents in parachute jumping, using explosives, writing in code, lock picking, and hand-to-hand combat.

The author Ian Fleming is believed to have trained at Camp X, leading some to conclude that the camp is the birthplace of Fleming's most famous character, James Bond 007.

DID YOU KNOW?

Canada has been free of weapons of mass destruction since 1984.

16

FUN FOOD & DRINK FACTS

UNIQUELY CANADIAN

POUTINE. French fries, fresh cheese curds (also called "squeaky cheese"), and brown gravy are the three ingredients that make up the classic dish.

Poutine was created in the province of Quebec and it's now considered one of Canada's signature foods. In Quebec, you may even find it as a side at a McDonald's or Burger King.

Pro tip:
Poutine is pronounced "Poo tin," rather than "Poo teen" and it's best when you have equal amounts of cheese and gravy.

BUTTER TARTS. Butter tarts are 100% Canadian and some think they were created as far back as the 1600s.

This sweet dessert is traditionally made with butter, sugar, maple or corn syrup and egg and are baked in a small pastry shell until the filling is firm with a crunchy top.

They are considered a national treasure, especially in Ontario, where you can take a self-guided butter tart tour to over 50 bakeries at any time of the year.

There are many different recipes when it comes to butter tarts, but here is a favorite: https://www.littlesweetbaker.com/butter-tarts/

NANAIMO BARS. Three layers of goodness make up this sweet no-bake iconic Canadian dessert.

The bottom layer is made of a coconut and graham crust, the middle is a soft, yellow custard, and topped with chocolate ganache.

It's called Nanaimo bars because it was invented from the city of Nanaimo in British Columbia on Vancouver Island.

If you wanted to give them a try without making the trip to Canada, here's the recipe found on the city of Nanaimo's website: https://www.nanaimo.ca/about-nanaimo/nanaimo-bars

Pro tip:
Nanaimo bars are always best served cold.

BEAVER TAILS. A flattened out, hole-free, doughnut that resembles the tail of a beaver with a variety of toppings and fillings and is served hot. There are over 120 possible topping combos, but cinnamon and sugar is the original.

To make your own, try this tried-and-true recipe: https://www. allrecipes.com/recipe/213590/theras-canadian-fried-dough/

KETCHUP CHIPS
Ketchup flavored potato chips can only be found in Canada and is a favorite snack among many Canadians.

CANADIAN FAVORITES

MAC & CHEESE. Canadians love their mac & cheese. They eat more Kraft macaroni and cheese than any other nation in the world.

It's often called Kraft Dinner or even KD for short and is the most popular items sold in grocery stores in the country.

Out of the 7 million boxes sold weekly around the world, Canadians purchase 1.7 million of them. This means around 88.4 million boxes a year.

COFFEE & DOUGHNUTS. Coffee is Canada's number one beverage with the average coffee drinker consuming 2.6 cups of coffee a day.

Where there's coffee, there's usually doughnuts and Canadians love their doughnuts. Canada eats the most doughnuts in the world and and has the most doughnut shops per capita of any country.

Tim Hortons, aka Timmies, is the most popular doughnut chain in Canada with over 2,500 shops selling over 3 million doughnuts a day.

Although the doughnut is seen as an American icon and was invented in America in 1847, it has become Canada's unofficial national snack.

TIMBIT. The Tim Hortons' Timbit is a play on the word "tidbit" and is another name for a doughnut hole.

The name comes from the crazy popular Tim Horton chain aka Timmies, that is known for their doughnuts and coffee.

Popular timbit flavors include apple cider, chocolate-glazed, the honey dip, pumpkin spice, cherry cake, and birthday cake.

MILK IN BAGS. Milk used to come in heavy glass bottles and in 1967, Canada started using plastic bags instead.

Bagged milk is more practical and cost-effective and Canada isn't the only country with bagged milk, but it's not something many Americans have seen.

FUN CANADIAN MAPLE SYRUP FACTS

CANADA IS KING WHEN IT COMES TO MAKING MAPLE SYRUP. More than 75% of the maple syrup in the world is made in Quebec, Canada.

Other regions where syrup is made include Ontario, New Brunswick, Prince Edward Island, and Nova Scotia.

NOT ALL MAPLE TREES ARE USED FOR SYRUP. Only three of the 10 types of maple trees native to Canada produce the sweet sap that is then boiled down to make the famous syrup. These are the Sweet Maple, Red Maple, and Black Maple trees.

TREES NEED TO BE A CERTAIN AGE. A maple tree needs to be at least 45 years old before it can be tapped for the sap that is used to make syrup.

100 YEARS. Once a maple tree starts producing sap, it can produce sap for more than a century.

A LOT TO MAKE A LITTLE. It takes about 10.5 gallons or 40 liters of sap to make just 1 liter or .25 gallons of syrup.

SNOW + MAPLE SYRUP = MAPLE TAFFY. Maple syrup isn't just for pancakes. Maple syrup is boiled past the point of syrup, but before it turns into maple butter.

It can then be poured on clean white snow for a treat. The cold snow causes the hot syrup to thicken and turns to a candy Canadians call Maple Taffy.

IN CASE OF EMERGENCY. Canada has more than 100 million pounds of maple syrup stored away in case there is a shortage of syrup.

This surplus makes it possible to stabilize syrup prices if there was ever a shortage.

UNIQUE CANADIAN CANDY

CHOCOLATE BARS NOT CANDY BARS. What Americans call candy bars, Canadians call chocolate bars, because they're mostly made of chocolate.

COFFEE CRISP

Coffee Crisp is a Canadian favorite and is unique to Canada. Vanilla wafers and a creamy coffee center covered in milk chocolate make this one of the most popular chocolate bars in Canada.

AERO

These Nestlé chocolate bars are filled with little air bubbles and then covered in smooth milk chocolate.

CARAMILK

Cadbury makes these caramel filled chocolate bars in Toronto.

The U.S., Australia, New Zealand, and the U.K. have similar bars, like the Cadbury Dairy Milk Caramel or Cadbury's Caramello, but there's only one Caramilk and it's Canadian.

CRUNCHIE

A crunchy, honeycomb toffee covered in milk chocolate make these Cadbury chocolate bars a favorite in Canada, the U.K., Australia, and New Zealand.

WUNDERBAR

Peanut butter lovers tend to love this bar that has a crushed roasted peanut caramel center covered in milk chocolate.

In Canada and Germany, it goes by the name of Wunderbar,

which means "marvelous" in German. In Ireland, Sweden, and Finland, you'll find it under the name of Starbar.

GLOSETTES
Chocolate-covered raisins aren't unique to Canada, but Glosettes are found in almost every movie theater in Canada.

SMARTIES
Canada has its own version of the candy-coated chocolate candies that Americans know as M&Ms. Across the border, they're called Smarties.

ROCKETS
Rockets are sweet, chalky candy circles that are known as "Smarties" in America.

WHERE TO FIND ONLINE
If you're not headed to Canada anytime soon, you can still find Canadian sweets online.

Here's where you can get your Canadian goodies:

- CanadianSweets.com
- CanadianMunch.com
- CandyFunHouse.ca
- Amazon - bit.ly/canadian-candy

DID YOU KNOW?
CANADIANS INVENTED HAWAIIAN PIZZA, NOT HAWAIIANS

This pineapple and ham topped pizza was invented in Canada in 1962. It is the most popular pizza in Australia and among the least liked pizza in the U.S.

17

FILMED IN CANADA

HOLLYWOOD NORTH. Vancouver is also known as Hollywood North. Canada's very own Hollywood is second to Los Angeles, California in TV production and third in North America for producing feature films.

MOVIES FILMED IN CANADA

This is just a list of some of the most famous movies filmed, at least in part, in Canada.

ONE WEEK (2008) - Epic motorcycle journey from Toronto through the Prairies and the Canadian Rockies, to Vancouver Island. Many of Canada's "Big Attractions" including Sudbury's nickel, Drumheller's dinosaur, and Wawa's Canada Goose make appearances.

BLADES OF GLORY (2007) - Filmed in Montreal, Quebec.

CAPOTE (2005) - Filmed in Winnipeg, Selkirk, Manitoba.

CATCH ME IF YOU CAN (2002) - Filmed the "European" scenes in Montréal and Quebec City.

COOL RUNNINGS (1993) - Loosely based on a true story about a Jamaican bobsled team competing in the 1998 Olympics in Calgary. To stay true to the story, much of the film was shot in Calgary.

FINDING FORRESTER (2000) - Filmed mainly in Brooklyn, Manhattan, and the Bronx in New York, but Toronto and Hamilton were used for scenery shots.

GOOD WILL HUNTING (1996) - Filmed in Toronto and Boston.

INCEPTION (2010) - Filmed all over the world, but several scenes shot in Alberta.

INTERSTELLAR (2014) - Filmed in several locations in Alberta.

MEAN GIRLS (2004) - Filmed in Toronto, Ontario.

MY BIG FAT GREEK WEDDING (2002) - Filmed in Toronto.

PIRATES OF THE CARIBBEAN: AT THE WORLD'S END (2006) - The epic, apocalyptic-style falls were actually the Canadian Horseshoe Falls side of Niagara Falls.

THE DAY AFTER TOMORROW (2004) - Highest-grossing Hollywood movie ever filmed in Canada, mainly filmed in Toronto and Montreal.

THE INCREDIBLE HULK (2008) - Filmed in Toronto, Ontario.

TITANIC (1997) - Filmed in Halifax, Nova Scotia.

TWILIGHT (2008) - Filmed in Vancouver and the Lower Mainland, British Columbia.

STRANGE BREW (1983) - This fun and quirky movie was filmed mainly in Ontario.

SUPERMAN (1978) - Filmed in Calgary and other parts of Alberta. The Fortress of Solitude was filmed in the British Columbian Icefields.

SUPERMAN II (1980) - Filmed in Calgary and Niagara Falls, Ontario.

SUPERMAN III (1983) - Filmed in several locations, but many scenes were shot in Calgary, like the previous two Superman films.

X-MEN: DAYS OF FUTURE PAST (2014) - Filmed in Montreal, Quebec.

TV SHOWS FILMED IN CANADA

This is far from a complete list of TV shows that have been filmed in Canada. This is just a list of some of the most famous.

ARROW (2012 -) - Filmed in Vancouver and in other parts of British Columbia.

CORNER GAS (2004 – 2009) The show is not only set in a small town in Saskatchewan, but it is also filmed in Saskatchewan.

FRINGE (2008 - 2013) - Filmed in Toronto and in Vancouver.

GILMORE GIRLS (2000 - 2007) - Filmed in Toronto, Ontario.

LUCIFER (2015 -) - The pilot was filmed in Los Angeles and subsequent episodes were filmed in Vancouver.

MACGYVER (1985 - 1992) - The first three seasons were shot in Los Angeles, and seasons three through six were all filmed in and around Vancouver.

ONCE UPON A TIME (2011 - 2018) - The fairytale show is set in the fictional town of Storybrooke, Maine. Filming took place in Steveston, not far from Vancouver.

PSYCH (2006 - 2014) - The show is set in Santa Barbara, California, but is actually filmed in Vancouver.

SMALLVILLE (2001 - 2011) - Shot in and around Vancouver.

SUPERNATURAL (2005 -) - Shot in Vancouver and other parts of British Columbia.

THE X-FILES (1993 - 2001 & 2016) - The first five seasons and the 2016 reboot were all filmed in Vancouver.

DID YOU KNOW?

Two of the stars in the original Star Trek TV show, William Shatner, who played Captain Kirk, and James Doohan, who played Scotty, were Canadian.

18

FAMOUS CANADIANS

MOVIE & TV STARS

RYAN GOSLING - Born in Ontario and is best known for acting in "La La Land" (2016) and "The Notebook" (2004).

He was the first Canadian-born performer to be nominated for a best actor Oscar award in 60 years.

RYAN REYNOLDS - Ryan was born in Vancouver and is known for playing opposite Sandra Bullock in "The Proposal" (2009) and the lead in the "Deadpool" (2016) movies.

He has a fear of flying that stems from a skydiving incident where his parachute didn't open on the first attempt.

KEANU REEVES - Keanu was not born in Canada, but moved to Toronto, Ontario when he was a teenager. His first name means, "cool breeze over the mountains" in Hawaiian.

He's known for "The Matrix" (1999), "Speed" (1994), and "Point Break" (1991).

JOHN CANDY - He was born in Toronto, Ontario and is considered one of Canada's funniest and greatest actors.

He is known for his roles in "Planes, Trains, and Automobiles" (1987), "Cool Runnings" (1993), "Spaceballs" (1987) and "Home Alone" (1990).

RICK MORANIS - Rick was born in Toronto, Ontario and is known for his roles in "The Ghostbusters" (1984), and "Honey, I Shrunk the Kids" (1989).

The role of Louis Tully in Ghostbusters was originally written for John Candy, but he dropped out and Rick was brought in at the last minute.

TAYLOR KITSCH - He's probably best known as playing Tim Riggins in "Friday Night Lights" (2006 - 2011) and the lead in "John Carter" (2012).

Taylor was born in British Columbia and played ice hockey for the Langley Hornets in the BCHL, but had to stop due to a knee injury in 2002.

EVANGELINE LILLY - Evangeline is best known for playing Kate in the TV show, "Lost" (2004 – 2010), Hope van Dyne/The Wasp in "Ant Man" (2015), and Tauriel in The Hobbit movies.

She was born in Fort Saskatchewan, Alberta. She is fluent in French and was discovered in Alberta by a modeling agent for Ford.

SANDRA OH - Sandra's parents are Korean, but she was born in Ontario. She is fluent in Korean, French, Spanish, and English. She is best known for playing Dr. Christina Yang in "Grey's Anatomy" (2005 – 2014).

NATHAN FILLION - Nathan was born in Edmonton, Alberta and is known for his lead roles in "Firefly" (2002 – 2003), "Castle" (2009 – 2016), and his latest show, "The Rookie" (2018 -).

His parents and brother are all teachers and Nathan originally wanted to be a high school drama teacher.

JIM CARREY - He is a dual citizen of both Canada and the U.S., but is a native Canadian born in Ontario. He's best known for "The Truman Show" (1998), "Dumb and Dumber" (1994), and "The Mask" (1994).

NIA VARDALOS - She was born in Winnipeg, Manitoba and is known for "My Big Fat Greek Wedding" (2002), "My Big Fat Greek Wedding 2" (2016), and "My Big Fat Greek Life" (2003).

My Big Fat Greek Wedding was originally a one-woman play. Tom Hanks' wife, Rita Wilson, saw it and recommended the play be made into a movie.

WILLIAM SHATNER - He's best known for his role as Captain James T. Kirk in the original Star Trek TV show. He was born in Montreal, Quebec and is fluent in French.

JAMES DOOHAN - He was born in Vancouver, British Columbia and is known as playing Scotty in the original Star Trek movies and TV show.

FAMOUS MUSICIANS

CÉLINE DION - Céline is known as the best-selling Canadian music artist and one of the best-selling music artists of all time. Her records have sold more than 200 million copies.

She is the youngest of 14 children and was born in the small town of Charlemagne, Quebec. Some of her best-selling songs are "Because You Loved Me," "It's All Coming Back to Me Now," and her signature song that has sold more than 15 million copies, "My Heart Will Go On."

MICHAEL BUBLÉ - He was born in British Columbia and dreamed of becoming a singer since he was a small boy. His big break came while singing at a wedding.

His song "Haven't Met You Yet" is actually a song about his wife, who stars in the music video as herself. Other songs he's known for are "Home" and "Sway."

JUSTIN BIEBER - He was born and raised in Ontario and is one of the best-selling artists globally. He was discovered singing covers on YouTube. He can play the piano, guitar, trumpet, and drums.

As of 2016, he has 14 records in the Guinness Book of World Records. A few worth noting are, "the most viewed music YouTube channel by an individual," "the most streamed track on Spotify in one week," and the "most followers on Twitter by a male."

SHANIA TWAIN - Known as "Queen of Country Pop," Shania

has sold more than 100 million albums and is known as the best-selling female country artist of all time.

She was born in Ontario and as part of the 2010 Olympic Torch Relay, she carried the Olympic torch through her hometown.

BRYAN ADAMS - One of his greatest hits "(Everything I Do) I Do It For You," was written for the movie, "Robin Hood: Prince of Thieves" (1991), in just 45 minutes.

Not only is he a singer, songwriter, and record producer, but he's a professional photographer. In 2002, the Canadian 49-cent stamp was of a candid photo he shot of Queen Elizabeth in Buckingham Palace.

THE BARENAKED LADIES - They are a Canadian indie rock band and despite their name, the band is made up of all guys. Some of their biggest hits include "One Week," "Pinch Me," and "If I Had $1000000."

ALANIS MORISSETTE - She was born in Ontario and was named "Queen of Alt-Rock Angst" by *Rolling Stone* magazine.

She was a child actor turned musician who released her first single when she was only 10 years old.

She has sold more than 75 million records and some of her best-selling songs include "Ironic," "Hand In My Pocket," and "You Learn."

AVRIL LAVIGNE - She won a radio contest to sing with Shania Twain in front of 20,000 people when she was only 15 years old.

At the age of 18, she broke the Guinness World Record to

become the youngest female solo artist to top the UK album charts.

She had a skate punk image and earned the nickname "Pop Punk Queen." Some of her biggest hits include, "Complicated," "Sk8er Boi," and "Girlfriend."

RUSH - Known as one of the most popular rock bands in the world, Rush had been around for more than 40 years and sold more than 40 million records.

The band got together in Toronto in the summer of 1968, but as of January 2018, they have officially disbanded.

They are known for their complex compositions and lyrics that draw from philosophy and science fiction.

They rank third after The Beatles and The Rolling Stones for the most consecutive gold and platinum albums by a rock band.

STEPPENWOLF - This Canadian-American rock band began as Jack London and The Sparrows who formed in Toronto, Ontario. After Jack London left the band, John Kay joined the Sparrows, and it became John Kay and The Sparrows.

After little success, the band disbanded and Jack moved to L.A. He recruited a few of the ex-Sparrow band members and a few new band members and named the band Steppenwolf after a popular novel.

Some of their biggest hits were "Born to Be Wild," "Magic Carpet Ride," and "Rock Me."

THE GUESS WHO - Originally known as The Silvertones and

then The Reflections, this Winnipeg band became one of the greatest Canadian rock bands in the late 1960s and early 1970s.

Some of their most successful songs were "American Woman," "No Time," and "These Eyes."

FAMOUS CANADIAN AUTHORS

LUCY MAUD MONTGOMERY - Her charming "Anne of Green Gables" novel series made her famous worldwide.

During her lifetime, she published 20 novels, 500 short-stories, 500 poems, and 30 essays with most of them set in Prince Edward Island. She chose to be published as L.M. Montgomery so readers wouldn't know what gender she was.

Her books put Prince Edward Island on the map and the town of Cavendish, which inspired the books, receives more than 125,000 tourists a year.

Many of the visitors are from Japan, where Anne of Green Gables is known as "Red-Haired Anne." Many Japanese couples travel to Prince Edward Island to be married in the house where Montgomery grew up.

Since 1952, the Anne of Green Gables books have been a staple of school curriculum and she is considered one of the most beloved fictional characters.

Quotes by L.M. Montgomery:

"Tomorrow is always fresh, with no mistakes in it." - "Anne of Green Gables"

"It's been my experience that you can nearly always enjoy things if you make up your mind firmly that you will." - "Anne of Green Gables"

MARGARET ATWOOD - She is considered one of Canada's best-known writers.

She was born in Ottawa and is known internationally for her award-winning poetry, short stories, and novels.

Some of her most notable works are "The Handmaid's Tale" (1985), "The Circle Game" (1966), "The Blind Assassin" (2000), and "The Tent" (2006). Many of her works have been adapted to film and television.

Atwood is also a talented photographer and watercolorist and on some occasions she has designed her own book covers.

She also invented the LongPen, a device that allows a person to remotely write in ink using a robotic hand, the Internet, and a PC tablet.

Quotes by Margaret Atwood:

"A word after a word after a word is power." - "Spelling"

"In the spring, at the end of the day, you should smell like dirt." - "Bluebeard's Egg"

YANN MARTEL - He is best known for his best-selling book "The Life of Pi" (2001). The novel won the Booker Prize, was translated into 30 languages, and was adapted into an Oscar-winning movie.

His first language is French, but he prefers to write in English.

As a child, he moved around a lot. He's lived in Canada, Mexico, Costa Rica, the United States, and France. As an adult he has lived in Iran, India, and Turkey.

Before turning to writing, he worked in a variety of odd jobs including tree planter, security guard, and dishwasher.

Quotes by Yann Martel:

> *"It is true that those we meet can change us, sometimes so profoundly that we are not the same afterwards, even unto our names."* - "The Life of Pi"

ALICE MUNRO - Alice is considered a legendary short-story writer. She was 82 when she won the Nobel Prize in Literature, making her the first Canadian and 13th woman ever to receive it.

She grew up in Ontario and has written short stories since 1950.

She knew she wanted to be a writer when she was 14. She always wanted to write a novel, but as a mother she found she didn't have time and decided to write short stories instead. She would think about and piece the stories together during her children's naps.

Quotes by Alice Munro:

"That's something I think is growing on me as I get older: happy endings."

"The constant happiness is curiosity."

STEPHEN LEACOCK - He was once the best-known English speaking humorist in the world.

At one point it is said that more people had heard of Stephen Leacock than Canada and he was one of the most widely-read authors in the English-speaking world.

He was a teacher, writer, lecturer, and humorist who wrote more than 30 books of lighthearted essays and sketches. Many of his articles were published in Canadian and American magazines.

He wrote biographies on both Mark Twain and Charles Dickens. His best-known books of humorous sketches are *"Literary Lapses"* (1910) and *"Nonsense Novels"* (1911).

As a tribute, the Stephen Leacock Medal for Humour was created. This prestigious literary award is presented annually to the best book of humor. It's one of the oldest literary awards in Canada and the only one awarded to a work of humor.

Quotes by Stephen Leacock:

"I am a great believer in luck, and I find the harder I work, the more I have of it."

"Life, we learn too late, is in the living, in the tissue of every day and hour."

MARGARET LAURENCE - Many of Margaret's novels and short stories have become classics in Canadian literature.

She was born in Manitoba, but lived in Ghana, Somaliland (now Somalia), England, and Canada, where she returned at the end of her life.

Her writings were influenced by her experiences, especially in Africa, and often portrayed strong women and their daily struggle to make a living and a life in a male-dominated world.

She is best known for her novel "The Stone Angel." It was the first of five books set in a fictional Canadian town called Manawaka. "The Stone Angel" was at one time required reading in many schools in North America and was made into a film in 2007.

Quotes by Margaret Laurence:

> *"It would be nice if we were different people but we are not different people. We are ourselves and we are sure as hell not going to undergo some total transformation at this point."* - "The Fire-Dwellers"

> *"Too bad to deprive them, but if a person doesn't look after herself in this world, no one else is likely to."* - "The Stone Angel"

PIERRE BERTON - This historian, journalist, host of his own TV show, and author of fifty books in fifty years was born in Whitehorse, Yukon in 1920.

He grew up working in Klondike mining camps and then attended the Royal Military College in Ontario where he learned journalism. He became the youngest news editor of a Canadian daily paper in 1942.

He's best known for writing about Canadian history for adults, youth, and children in an understandable and engaging way. Many of his books are now considered Canadian classics.

He was famous for his bow ties, conducting the only surviving television interview with the famous martial artist Bruce Lee, and having an award for those who present Canadian history in an informative and engaging manner named after him.

Quotes by Pierre Berton:

"I only write books about dead people. They can't sue."

"My best advice to writers is get yourself born in an interesting place."

OTHER FAMOUS CANADIANS

WAYNE GRETZKY, HOCKEY PLAYER - Ontario native Wayne Gretzky has earned the nickname "The Great One."

He's considered to be the greatest hockey player ever. Wayne Gretzky has scored more goals and completed more assists than anyone in NHL history before or since.

He is the only NHL player who has ever scored more than 200 points in one season, and he did it a jaw-dropping four different times.

He is the only player who has had his jersey number, 99, retired league-wide by the NHL.

He had a skill for dodging body checks from other players, anticipating where the puck would be, and being ready to make the right plays at the right time.

Here are two of his most famous quotes:

> *"A good hockey player plays where the puck is. A great hockey player plays where the puck is going to be."*

> *"You miss 100 percent of the shots you never take."*

CHRIS HADFIELD, ASTRONAUT - Chris was the first Canadian to walk in space, the first to operate the Canadarms, and the country's first commander of the International Space Station.

One of many things that made him famous was performing and recording himself playing David Bowie's "Space Oddity" while in space.

He and William Shatner, known as the Enterprise space captain in Star Trek, chatted on Twitter while he was in space.

Chris is also one of eight astronauts featured in the TV documentary series "One Strange Rock" (2018 -).

JAMES CAMERON, FILM MAKER - If you've seen or heard of the movies, "Titanic" (1997), "Avatar" (2009), "The Terminator" (1984), and "True Lies" (1994) you've seen the work of James Cameron.

He's from Ontario and is not only a famous, record-breaking filmmaker, but is also a deep-sea explorer. He is one of only three people in the world who has explored the deepest part of the Mariana Trench in the Pacific Ocean.

DRAKE, RAPPER AND ACTOR - Drake started out as an actor in the Canadian teen TV show, "Degrassi: The Next Generation" (2001 – 2009). He played the wheelchair-bound Jimmy Brooks for seven years before moving on to a career in music.

Shortly after releasing his first mixtape, he received a call from the American rapper Lil Wayne, who invited Drake to join his tour.

This was the beginning of an impressive music career that includes breaking records set by Michael Jackson and Justin Bieber.

WOLVERINE, CANADIAN COMIC BOOK HERO - This popular and much-loved fictional character is from Canada, according to the original Marvel comic books that inspired the X-Men franchise.

19

MYTHS, FOLKLORE, & WEIRD

CANADA'S VERY OWN LOCH NESS MONSTER. In Canadian folklore, there's a mythical creature called Ogopogo living in the Okanagan Lake in British Columbia.

Ogopogo means "spirit of the lake" and refers to a lake monster, similar to Scotland's Loch Ness Monster. The creature has been described as a sea serpent that is 40 to 50 feet long or 12 to 15 meters.

GRAVITY LEVELS. Large areas of Canada, especially around the Hudson Bay region, have lower levels of gravity than the rest of Earth. This means that people weigh less here than anywhere else on earth, though the effect is barely noticeable unless measured.

According to scientists, this area was covered by the Laurentide Ice Sheet over 10,000 years ago. The ice sheet was so massive, that it left a deep indentation which caused gravity to bend.

The area is slowly rebounding, but will take close to 5,000 years until it flattens out and gravity in that area returns to normal.

UFO PARKING. St Paul, Alberta built the world's first landing pad for UFOs. Is it a coincidence that the X-Files TV show was filmed in Canada?

SAILORS DON'T WEAR GRAY GLOVES. Superstitious Canadian sailors refuse to wear gray gloves. Undertakers traditionally wore gray gloves and some believe wearing them is like issuing an invitation to death.

RED SKIES MEANT WINDY DAYS. During the Depression, farmers in the province of Saskatchewan believed that if the skies turned red, the following day's weather would be too windy to plant.

DEVIL'S BERRIES. In Alberta, some people believe that it's bad luck to pick blackberries after October 11th. After the 11th, they believe the berries belong to the devil and should be left alone.

BAD LUCK TO WASH DISHES. In the Canadian Prairies, if a neighbor brings a dish of food, the plate should be returned dirty and unwashed. It is believed to bring bad luck otherwise.

LOONIE FOR GOOD LUCK. At the Salt Lake 2002 Winter Olympics, a Loonie, a Canadian $1 coin, was put under the ice on the face-off dot of the hockey rink for good luck. Both the Canadian men's and women's hockey teams won gold medals.

The tradition continues today, including at the Vancouver Olympics in 2010.

20

CANADA'S FAMOUS ATTRACTIONS

3-IN-1 WATERFALL AKA NIAGARA FALLS. Three different waterfalls make up Niagara Falls:

- **American Falls** - named because it's mostly over the U.S. border.
- **Bridal Veil Falls** - the smallest of the three falls gets its name because it resembles a brides veil.
- **Horseshoe Falls aka Canadian Falls** - the largest and tallest of the falls is mostly in Ontario and shaped like a horseshoe.

These waterfalls are **split between Canada and the U.S.** through two cities that share the same name. On one side is Niagara Falls, Ontario and the other, Niagara Falls, New York. The falls can be seen from both sides.

Niagara Falls is one of the world's most visited attractions, with more than 30 million visitors a year. It's also the **world's most popular honeymoon destinations** and has been for more than 200 years.

In 1901, on her 63rd birthday, a retired school teacher named **Annie Taylor was the first person to go over the falls** and survive.

Annie had a custom barrel made with an air hole drilled at the top, straps installed to keep her in place, and a 200 -pound or 90-kilogram anvil at the bottom to allow the barrel to stay upright.

To test the barrel before her big event, she put a cat inside and sent it over the falls. The cat and barrel both survived, so Annie went ahead and made her big splash. According to legend the cat was black when it went into the barrel, but was scared so bad that after the fall it came out white.

For those adrenaline junkies who want to give it a go, you'll find it's now illegal and comes with a $10,000 fine.

The word Niagara comes from the Iroquois word "Onguiaahra," which means **"strait."**

CN TOWER OR CANADA'S NATIONAL TOWER. Once the tallest freestanding tower in the world, until 2007, the CN Tower is now the third-tallest tower in the world, but remains the tallest in the western hemisphere.

More than 1.5 million visitors come each year to check out one of the Seven Wonders of the Modern World.

The CN Tower is **struck by lightning** an average of 75 times per year. To prevent damage, long copper strips run down the length of the tower to grounding rods that are buried below ground.

Architects built the CN Tower to withstand extreme wind and

major earthquakes. It's **built to withstand an 8.5 earthquake** on the Richter scale and the upper parts of the tower are built to withstand winds up to 260 mph or 418 kph.

WORLD'S LARGEST COIN. The Big Nickel in Ontario is the world's largest coin. This nickel is 20 feet or 9.1 meters high and 2 feet or 0.61 meters thick.

This 5-cent coin is 64 million times larger than the real Canadian nickel and weighs almost 13,000 kilograms or 28,600 pounds. This 13-ton nickel is 94.5% steel, 3.5% copper, and 2% nickel.

WORLD'S LARGEST DINOSAUR REPLICA. The world's largest dinosaur replica can be found in Drumheller, Alberta.

Drumheller is famous for its large number of dinosaur bones and fossils. A Tyrannosaurus Rex replica stands at 4.5 times the size of a real T-Rex and visitors can climb into her mouth for an epic view of Alberta's Badlands.

WORLD'S LARGEST HOCKEY STICK. Weighing 61,000 lbs or 28,118 kgs and stretching 203 feet or 62 meters long, the world's largest hockey stick and puck can be seen in the city of Duncan, British Columbia. Now that's a hockey stick.

WORLD'S LARGEST INDOOR AMUSEMENT PARK. The largest indoor amusement park is in the West Edmonton Mall. This mall used to be the largest in the world and is now the fifth largest indoor mall.

CANADA'S LARGEST AMUSEMENT PARK. Canada's Wonderland is just north of Toronto and is the most visited seasonal amusement park in North America.

It's also tied for second with the Cedar Point amusement park with seventeen roller coasters, just after Six Flags Magic Mountain with nineteen coasters.

DID YOU KNOW?

The Eiffel Tower was almost relocated to Canada temporarily in 1967.

LEARN TO SPEAK CANADIAN

French and English are Canada's two official languages.

"Canadian English" is mostly British English and you'll notice a few words spelled slightly different than what is found in "American English."

For example, the letter "u" is used in words like colour and neighbour and center is spelled as centre.

FUN CANADIAN WORDS TO KNOW

Eh?
A word that means the same thing as "huh", "what?" and "right?" and is listed in the Canadian Oxford Dictionary as a valid word. Here's an example of how to use it in a sentence: "We're going to go get Timbits today, eh?"

Loonie

The Canadian $1 coin is called a loonie and it gets its name from the loon, a Canadian bird that appears on one side of the coin.

Toonie
The Canadian $2 coin is called a toonie to match the sound of the loonie.

Tuque
A knitted hat similar to what Americans call a beanie that is usually worn when it's cold. Pronounced "tuke."

Kerfuffle
A word that means a fuss or commotion, usually from a disagreement.

Knapsack or Rucksack
What Canadians call their backpacks.

Dart
A slang word for a cigarette.

Housecoat
It's what you wear around the house before getting dressed. Americans call it a bathrobe or if they're classy, a dressing gown.

Eavestroughs
A word for rain gutters found on houses.

Elastics
Americans call them rubber bands, but in Canada, they are called elastics.

Freezies

Heard of Otter Pops or Freeze Pops? In Canada, they're known as Freezies.

Garburator
Another word for a garbage disposal under a kitchen sink that grinds up food into small pieces to avoid clogging pipes.

KD
KD stands for Kraft Dinner, which Americans will know as Kraft macaroni and cheese.

Klick
Another way to refer to kilometers. One kilometer is about 0.6 miles. An example of how it's used: "The nearest hockey game is only two klicks away."

Molson muscle
Molson is the name of a popular beer in Canada, so this is another way of referring to a beer belly.

Parkade
Another way to refer to a parking garage.

Pencil crayons
Another word for colored pencils.

Queue (lineup)
A word used to refer to a line of people waiting for something. Queue and lineup mean the same thing and are both used.

Runners
Another word for running shoes, sneakers, tennis shoes, or even street shoes.

Hydro Bills
Americans pay their utility or electric bills, Canadians pay hydro bills.

Serviette
The word for napkins.

Snowbirds
Canadians who head south during the winter to get away from the cold are called snowbirds. Arizona and Florida are favorite hot spots.

Tap
Americans turn on the faucet to get water, but Canadians get water from the tap.

Thongs
The footwear you'd wear at the beach or the pool. Americans call them flip flops or sandals.

Toboggan and Tobogganing
Another word for a thin, light sled used to slide down a hill of snow during the winter. Most Americans call it a sled and go sledding. Canadians go tobogganing. Either way, it's a fun winter activity.

Timmies
The nickname for the much-loved doughnut and coffee chain, Tim Hortons, which is named after a famous Canadian hockey player.

Timbit
The Tim Hortons' Timbit is a play on the word "tidbit" and is another name for a doughnut hole. The name comes from the

crazy popular Tim Hortons chain known for their doughnuts and coffee.

Popular timbit flavors include apple cider, chocolate-glazed, the honey dip, pumpkin spice, cherry cake, and birthday cake.

Double-double
Regular coffee with two creams and two sugars.

Pop
Some people say soda, soft drink, or soda pop but in Canada it's pop.

Washroom
Canadians prefer to refer to it as a washroom, but other words for it are the "men's room," the "ladies' room," restrooms, bathrooms, water closet, the loo, or toilet.

Zed
This refers to the last letter in the English alphabet "Z." You can pronounce it as "Zee," but if you want to fit in, say it as "Zed."

22

ODD CANADIAN LAWS

COMIC BOOK CRIME. It's against the law to possess, print, publish or sell comic books that show any type of criminal act.

COLORFUL HOMES. In Beaconsfield, Quebec, you can be fined for painting your home with more than two different colors of paint.

NO COWS IN THE HOUSE. In Newfoundland, it's against the law to keep a cow in your home like a house pet. However, it is not illegal to own a cow.

FINES FOR NOISY PARROTS. If your pet parrot likes to talk loudly and you live in the Oak Bay neighborhood in Victoria, you could be fined $100.

DON'T SCARE THE QUEEN. According to the Canadian Criminal Code, it is illegal to scare the Queen.

This became a law around 1842, when a British man pointed a

gun at Queen Victoria, but did not shoot. It obviously scared her and a law was made.

NO SIRENS ON BICYCLES. While attaching a bell or horn to your bike is acceptable, adding a siren is illegal in Sudbury, Ontario and can cost you up to $5,000 in fines.

NO "WEARING" SNAKES IN PUBLIC. For those who like to "wear" snakes or lizards around your neck or other parts of your body in public, you're breaking the law in Fredericktown, New Brunswick.

You'll need a glass container to keep your snakes and other reptiles in while out in public.

SHH!! KEEP IT DOWN! An anti-noise law has banned "yelling, shouting, hooting, whistling or singing" between 11 p.m. and 7 a.m. in Petrolia, Ontario. You'll have to practice your whistling during the day.

NO PAINTING WOOD LADDERS. In Alberta, it's against the law to paint a wooden ladder. Why? If a ladder is old and rickety, a new coat of paint could disguise the condition and be a safety hazard.

BURIED IN SNOW. A law in Canada states that children must not be buried alive in snow deeper than six feet.

DON'T RIP OFF THE BANDAID. Citizens may not remove bandages in public. It's illegal in some parts of Canada and it grosses some people out.

NO POLAR BEAR BURGERS. It's illegal to make burgers out of polar bears.

ILLEGAL SPIT. In Montreal, it is illegal for citizens to urinate or spit on the street. Citizens will be fined over $100.

SWEARING.
In Montreal, it's illegal to swear in French.
In Quebec, it is illegal to curse in any language other than French.
In Toronto, it's illegal to swear at your mother in public.

SAVE WATER. In Nova Scotia, it's against the law to water your lawn while it's raining.

BEAR SPRAY IS LEGAL. PEPPER SPRAY IS NOT. In Canada, it's illegal to carry a product designed for personal protection against a human attack, including pepper spray and mace.

However, carrying bear spray is legal for use against bears.

23

NICKNAMES & MOTTOS FOR CANADA'S PROVINCES & TERRITORIES

EVERYONE LOVES A GOOD NICKNAME.

Here are a few official and unofficial nicknames and mottos.

CANADA

- **Great White North** - Probably the most common nickname, it refers to Canada as being big, north, and white due to most of the country experiencing long, sometimes harsh, winters.
- **Borealia -** In many parts of Canada, especially in rural places, the northern lights, also known as the aurora borealis, can be seen.
- **Canadia -** Word play on Canadians.

CANADIANS

- **Canucks** - A slang term for Canadians.

ALBERTA

- **Wild Rose Country** - The motto currently on license plates.
- **Berta**

BRITISH COLUMBIA

- **B.C.**
- **Super, Natural, British Columbia**
- **Beautiful British Columbia** - The motto currently on license plates.

MANITOBA

- **Friendly Manitoba** - The motto currently on license plates.
- **Land of 100,000 Lakes**
- **The Postage Stamp Province**

NEW BRUNSWICK

- **The Picture Province**
- **The Loyalist Province**

NEWFOUNDLAND AND LABRADOR

- **The Rock**
- **The Big Land (Labrador)**

NORTHWEST TERRITORIES

- **The Land of the Midnight Sun**
- **Land of the Polar Bear**
- **Canada's Last Frontier**

NOVA SCOTIA

- **Canada's Ocean Playground** - The mottos is currently on license plates.
- **The Sea Bound Coast**
- **Bluenoser Province**

NUNAVUT

- **The Land of the Midnight Sun**

ONTARIO

- **Yours to Discover** - The motto is currently on license plates.
- **The Heartland Province**

QUEBEC

- **La Belle Province (French for "The Beautiful Province")**
- **Je me souviens (French for "I remember")** - The motto currently on license plates.

PRINCE EDWARD ISLAND

- **P.E.I.**
- **The Island**
- **Spud Island** - Refers to the potatoes that are grown in the red, sandy soil found here and are the province's main cash crop.
- **Million Acre Farm** - The land area on the Island is over 1 million acres with much of it used to farm potatoes, grains, oilseeds, and fruit.

SASKATCHEWAN

- **The Bread Basket of Canada** - This comes from the fact that it is Canada's largest producer of grains and oilseeds.
- **The Land of Seed and Honey**
- **Land of the Living Skies** - The motto currently on license plates.

YUKON

- **The Land of the Midnight Sun**

24

QUOTABLES

"Canada has always been there to help people who need it." - Prime Minister Justin Trudeau

"I believe the world needs **more** Canada." - Bono, Musician

"Canada is the homeland of equality, justice and tolerance." - Former Prime Minister Kim Campbell

"Canada is like a loft apartment over a really great party." - Robin Williams, Comedian

"Canada is not a country for the cold of heart or the cold of feet." - Former Prime Minister Pierre Trudeau

"It is wonderful to feel the grandness of Canada in the raw." - Emily Carr, Author

"Canada is a great country, one of the hopes of the world." - Jack Layton, Politician

"Canada is one of the planet's most comfortable, and caring, societies. The United Nations Human Development Index listed the country as one of the most desirable places in the world to live." - *Time* magazine

"Canada is free and freedom is its nationality." - Former Prime Minister Wilfrid Laurier

"You look at the history - the aboriginal people welcomed the first settlers here with open arms, fed us and took care of us ... that continues today, we welcome people from all nations to come in and share." - Peter Stoffer, Politician

"I love being Canadian. I think growing up in Canada gives you a world perspective that I certainly enjoy." - Ryan Gosling, Actor

"We have it all. We have great diversity of people, we have a wonderful land, and we have great possibilities. So all those things combined there's nowhere else I'd rather be." - Bob Rae, Former Politician

"When I'm in Canada, I feel this is what the world should be like." - Jane Fonda, Actress

"I love Canada. It's a wonderful political act of faith that exists atop a breathtakingly beautiful land." - Yann Martel, Author

"Canada is one of the most impressive countries in the world." - Barack Obama, Former U.S. President

25

QUIZ YOURSELF

1. What's a Double Double?
   A. A hamburger with two patties
   B. A coffee
   C. A type of gum
   D. A type of point scored in a hockey game

2. What do you use a Toque for?
   A. To heat up your car
   B. As a flavoring
   C. To keep your head warm
   D. To sled down snowy hills

3. What is Canada's National Sport?
   A. Basketball
   B. Lacrosse
   C. Hockey
   D. Golf

. . .

4. Which potato chip flavor is unique to Canada?
   A. Maple
   B. Dill Pickle
   C. Poutine
   D. Ketchup

5. The Northwest Territories has a license plate shaped like what animal?
   A. Polar Bear
   B. Moose
   C. Goose
   D. Beaver

6. Which invention was NOT invented by a Canadian or in Canada?
   A. Snowmobile
   B. Garbage bags
   C. Basketball
   D. The Zamboni

7. Which comic book character was invented by a Canadian?
   A. Wonder Woman
   B. Spiderman
   C. The Hulk
   D. Superman

8. What is the tallest mountain in Canada?
   A. Mount Saint Elias
   B. Mount Vancouver

C. Mount Logan

D. Denali

9. In the movie, "Cool Runnings" what city do the Winter Olympics take place in?

A. Vancouver

B. Montreal

C. Calgary

D. Halifax

10. Which of these movie stars is NOT from Canada?

A. John Candy

B. Sandra Oh

C. Ryan Reynolds

D. Harrison Ford

11. Which of these famous singers is NOT from Canada?

A. Celine Dion

B. Ed Sheeran

C. Shania Twain

D. Justin Bieber

12. What is Canada's national animal?

A. Loon

B. Polar Bear

C. Moose

D. Beaver

13. Canadians celebrate Thanksgiving

A. True

B. False

14. Canadians eat more macaroni and cheese than any other country.

A. True

B. False

15. The Winnie the Pooh character was inspired by a female, black bear cub originally from Canada.

A. True

B. False

16. The Canadian $2 dollar coin is called a Loonie.

A. True

B. False

17. The Hawaiian Pizza was invented in Canada.

A. True

B. False

18. Which dessert is unique to Canada?

A. Neapolitan ice cream

B. Baked Alaska

C. Butter Tarts

D. Doughnut holes

19. A Smartie in Canada is what type of candy?

A. Chocolate covered raisins

B. Small, chalky discs that come in different colors

C. Candy-coated chocolate candies, similar to M&Ms

D. Small sucker that comes in different flavors

20. **What city is the capital of Canada?**

A. Calgary

B. Montreal

C. Vancouver

D. Ottawa

26

QUIZ ANSWERS

1. **What's a Double Double?**
   A. A hamburger with two patties
   B. A coffee
   C. A type of gum
   D. A type of point scored in a hockey game

2. **What do you use a Toque for?**
   A. To heat up your car
   B. As a flavoring
   C. To keep your head warm
   D. To sled down snowy hills

3. **What is Canada's National Sport?**
   A. Basketball
   B. Lacrosse
   C. Hockey
   D. Golf

· · ·

4. Which potato chip flavor is unique to Canada?

   A. Maple

   B. Dill Pickle

   C. Poutine

   D. Ketchup

5. The Northwest Territories has a license plate shaped like what animal?

   A. Polar Bear

   B. Moose

   C. Goose

   D. Beaver

6. Which invention was NOT invented by a Canadian or in Canada?

   A. Snowmobile

   B. Garbage bags

   C. Basketball

   D. The Zamboni

7. Which comic book character was invented by a Canadian?

   A. Wonder Woman

   B. Spiderman

   C. The Hulk

   D. Superman

8. What is the tallest mountain in Canada?

   A. Mount Saint Elias

   B. Mount Vancouver

C. Mount Logan

D. Denali

9. In the movie, "Cool Runnings" what city do the Winter Olympics take place in?

A. Vancouver

B. Montreal

C. Calgary

D. Halifax

10. Which of these movie stars is NOT from Canada?

A. John Candy

B. Sandra Oh

C. Ryan Reynolds

D. Harrison Ford

11. Which of these famous singers is NOT from Canada?

A. Celine Dion

B. Ed Sheeran

C. Shania Twain

D. Justin Bieber

12. What is Canada's national animal?

A. Loon

B. Polar Bear

C. Moose

D. Beaver

13. Canadians celebrate Thanksgiving

A. **True**
B. False

14. Canadians eat more macaroni and cheese than any other country.
   A. **True**
   B. False

15. The Winnie the Pooh character was inspired by a female, black bear cub originally from Canada.
   A. **True**
   B. False

16. The Canadian $2 dollar coin is called a Loonie.
   A. True
   B. **False**

17. The Hawaiian Pizza was invented in Canada.
   A. **True**
   B. False

18. Which dessert is unique to Canada?
   A. Neapolitan ice cream
   B. Baked Alaska
   C. **Butter Tarts**
   D. Doughnut holes

19. A Smartie in Canada is what type of candy?

A. Chocolate covered raisins

B. Small, chalky discs that come in different colors

C. Candy-coated chocolate candies, similar to M&Ms

D. Small sucker that comes in different flavors

20. What city is the capital of Canada?

A. Calgary

B. Montreal

C. Vancouver

D. Ottawa

LEARN SOMETHING? PLEASE LEAVE A REVIEW

If you enjoyed this book, please share your thoughts in a REVIEW. Your sincere feedback is really helpful and I would love to hear from you!

Please leave a quick review on
Amazon at
bit.ly/you-know-canada-book

If Goodreads is more your thing, please share it there.
www.goodreads.com

Thank you so very much!

DON'T FORGET YOUR FREE BONUS

As a **special bonus** and as a **thank you** for downloading this book, I created a **FREE companion quiz e-book** with **over 100 fun questions and answers** taken from this book.

How well DO YOU REALLY KNOW Canada?
Test your knowledge of Canada and quiz your friends.

It's all FREE.
Download your bonus quiz e-book here:

http://bit.ly/canada-bonus

Enjoy!

ABOUT THE AUTHOR

Marianne Jennings is a self-proclaimed adventure craver and an adventure addict. She is the Chief Adventure Officer of AdventureCravers.com, proudly holds the title of favorite aunt to her ten nieces and nephews, and is a lover of new foods and new experiences.

She loves facts and trivia like Canadians love maple syrup and hockey. To help introduce other places, people, and cultures to others, she likes to share interesting and fun facts that are entertaining and memorable.

If you'd like to learn more or join her mailing list, you can connect with Marianne at https://knowledgenuggetbooks.com or on Instagram.

instagram.com/knowledgenuggetbooks

Printed in Great Britain
by Amazon

66709807R00076